50/7

50 WORDS   **7 STEPS**

THE GOSPEL MESSAGE

THE HOLY BIBLE

??? ???? ???
?? FAITH ??

AN OVERALL VIEW OF EACH OF THE 3 ABOVE SUBJECTS IN 50 WORDS INTERTWINED INTO 7 STEPS.

E. L. "Eddie" Taylor

50/7
Fifty Words
Seven Steps

Copyright © 2008
All Rights Reserved

PUBLISHED BY:
BRENTWOOD CHRISTIAN PRESS
WWW.BRENTWOODBOOKS.COM
1-800-334-8861

50/7 ... What does it mean?

50 Words ... ... 7 Steps
But it means much more than 50 words and 7 steps.

50/7 is an overall view of these three subjects: The Holy Bible, The Gospel Message, Faith.

Each of the three subjects are narrowed into a foundation of 50 Words which then can be intertwined into 7 Steps.

50/7

Is a tool of simplicity...
for giving answer...
as to what one believes.

50/7 is dedicated to...

All who are in search of Truth, to affirm for self and to be ready to give answer to anyone who may ask of the reason of hope within.

Introduction

Welcome! My name is Eddie Taylor and I want to Thank You, for your interest to look into *50/7*.

May it help to give excellence of knowledge to the understanding as to what one may believe.

There are three parts to *50/7* and each is important to the other, yet each has a significance of its own. Any of the three can be taken in the order where one finds the greater interest. But the three intertwine together to give excellence of knowledge and bring oneness to *50/7* on:

The Holy Bible, as the question may be ask, is the Holy Bible the Blessed Book? or just another book?

The Gospel Message, what does it mean, as proclaimed through the Holy Bible on the life of Jesus Christ?

Faith, Where do we find ourselves to be in our own belief system of living through the substance of things hoped for?

Why is it often hard to share the answer as to what one might believe?

Is it that we might not be as sure of our answer as one should be? or that we get off of the thought and find it hard to get back on track? Or do we not keep it simple enough to speak with clarity and simplicity of answer?

To give a clear and precise answer as to what and why one believes in the manner in which they do. This is where *50/7* can help one to be more confident of what one believes on any subject.

50/7 can help one to stay on track with any subject, that one may feel the need to be shared. And do it in a simplistic manner, with clarity, and without a lot of personal opinion.

50/7 can help take self through what one thinks…to what one believes…and from what one believes…to what one knows. And to know that we know, that we know, that we know!

50/7 is a tool that begins with self. And self can proceed at its own pace, and in its own way, to bring forth in self that which one truly believes.

If I should ask, is the Holy Bible the Blessed Book? or just another book?

Would anyone care to share an answer?

If I were to ask, what does the Gospel Message mean? Would anyone care to reply with an answer?

Would anyone care to define Faith? or how we may obtain Faith?

I ask these questions with a purpose in mind. Did the questions give you pause to answer?

Did you decide not to answer even though you had an answer in mind as to how you could reply?

Are you fully confident in the thought you have or the answer you may have given?

In anything that one truly believes, it needs to be narrowed to the fewest words possible within the one that believes as they do, that they may know for themselves, WHY they believe in that manner.

The Holy Bible, the Gospel Message, and Faith are three very large subjects to be able to give an overall view through *50/7*.

Many questions are often asked on these three subjects, and many kinds of answers and opinions are often given of them.

But each of the three can stand on their own merit. Each of the three can in substance, be narrowed into 50 words to give a foundation for belief, and be clear with simplicity of answer.

Each of the three can intertwine with the other, to strengthen the knowledge, as to why one believes in the manner that is believed, for living out lives in the way that they are lived. And when we know for ourselves, then our own faith is affirmed, and we are then better able to share with others as opportunities present themselves.

For when we know for ourselves, a foundation of 50 words for sharing an overall view of the Holy Bible, or in giving answer on the Gospel Message, or in sharing an answer on Faith, we can share an answer as short as a minute, or as long as there is interest, or somewhere in between, depending upon the available time.

By knowing the 50 words, and treasuring them in our hearts, we can affirm them through scripture for ourselves and be ready to share with all who may ask of us, the reason of hope within, for living life as we do.

As we begin to look to *50/7* for an overall view answer to the question... Is the Holy Bible the Blessed Book or just another book, we may want to ask here of self, do I believe the Holy Bible to be the infallible Word of God?

Can we give answer as to WHY we believe? Or as to WHY we do not believe? Or WHY we may not be sure of what we believe the Holy Bible to be?

Let us now begin with an overall view of the Holy Bible, through *50/7*.

Section I

The Holy Bible
    The Blessed Book
        or just another book?

Here are 50 words that may be used in answer to an overall view of The Holy Bible.

Written over a period of fifteen hundred plus years, forty writers penned the words out of:
    Different backgrounds;
      Different vocations;
        Different times;
Prophecies proclaimed hundreds of years earlier fulfilled in Jesus Christ, bringing together one theme, the redemptive plan of God, for mankind through Jesus Christ as Savior and Lord.

We can now bring the 50 words into 7 steps.

(At this point, I would like to say that anything in Italic type that has been written are my comments and thoughts, while each word in Times New Roman regular type is taken from the Holy Bible.)

Step 1 - Written over some fifteen hundred plus years, the first five books of the Holy Bible; Genesis, Exodus, Leviticus, Numbers, and Deuteronomy, are accredited to be the writings of Moses in the time of 1460 B. C. - 1410 B. C., the last book of the Holy Bible, the book of the Revelations was written down by St. John on the isle of Patmos between 68 A. D. -97 A. D., so the 1460 years of old testament times and the 68 to 97 years of new testament times added together bring the times in which the Holy Bible was written to fifteen hundred plus years.

Step 2 - Over this 1500 plus years period of time, some forty different writers were inspired to write in the manner which they wrote. We can read in (Hebrews 1:1, 2) God who at sundry (different) times, and in divers (various) manners, spake in time past unto the fathers by the prophets, hath in these last days spoken unto us by His Son, whom He hath appointed heir of all things, by whom also He made the worlds.

In (II Peter 1:21) we can read, For the prophecy came not in old time by the will of man:

but holy men of God spake as they were moved by the Holy Ghost.

These forty men were born of different times throughout the 1500 plus years in which the Holy Bible was written. They came from all walks of life; some were kings ... others were shepherds... one a tax collector.., another a doctor... another a tent-maker, ...some were fishermen, and yet over this long period of time of some 1500 plus years, with the many different vocations that came forth out of the many back-grounds, **it** *all comes together to reveal the love of God; His grace and mercy, upon His creation of mankind.*

Step 3 - *Prophecies were proclaimed, and then fulfilled hundreds of years later. The prophets (writers) were inspired to write (prophecy) of the coming Messiah, and we find these prophecies fulfilling hundreds of years later in the life of Jesus Christ, here on earth.*

Step 4 - *Prophecies concerning the birth of the Messiah are fulfilled in the gospel of St. Luke, chapters one and two; the gospel of Matthew chapter 1:18-25 and the gospel of St. John chapter one.*

Some 700 years before the birth of Christ, Isaiah prophesied the virgin birth. (Isaiah 7:14) Micah, some 500 years before it is to take place, tells in

Micah 5:2 of the city of Bethlehem, where the Messiah would be born. Malachi 3:1 we can read of the prophecy of the forerunner that is to come and prepare the way of the Lord some 400 years before *it* is to come to pass.

These three prophecies, we will take a closer look at in a moment, but we also want to say here that many other prophecies concerning the life, death, burial, and resurrection of the Messiah are recorded in the Holy Bible and revealed and fulfilled in the life of Jesus Christ as He came according to holy scripture.

Step 5 - *This can bring substance to our faith.* To see the supernatural ways of events in the life of Jesus Christ here on earth, defies our reasoning; defies our logic. As we learn more of Him, we can have faith beyond our own understanding, for *it* is not a blind faith but one based upon the evidence of things not seen, yet revealed by the Word of God; revealed through the Holy Spirit of God.

Step 6 - *It is revealed to us, a more excellent knowledge,* given to us through the Holy Spirit of God. We can know of the love of God for us even in the deepest times of sorrows; through our greatest adversities, we can know He is a very present help in the times of our trouble...

We can know of His great love for us...
and yet ...not know Him.

To know Him, comes through our own freewill to do so, we can receive Him or reject Him by the personal decision we make as to whether or not to receive Him into our heart and life. What have we done... or what will we do... with this one called Jesus?

Step 7 - *We can know that through His great love and mercies He has so freely bestowed upon us through and by His marvelous and sufficient grace, we can go forth to teach the oneness of the one true Triune God. He gives us this commission in Matthew 28:19, 20.*

Go ye therefore, and teach all nations, baptizing them in the name of the Father, and of the Son, and of the Holy Ghost: teaching them to observe all things whatsoever I have commanded you: and lo, I am with you alway, even unto the end of the world.

We can also read in the gospel of St. John 14:31 where Jesus spoke these words.

But that the world may know that I love the Father; and as the Father gave me commandment, even so I do. Arise let us go hence.

*We now want to take 50/7 and apply **it** to an overall view of the Holy Bible.*

Let us begin by taking a closer look at the gospel of St. Luke, chapters one and two and build upon the 50 words and seven steps. We will also look at the gospel of St. Matthew 1:18-25 and the gospel of St. John chapter one to see how they unfold to us.

Section II

50/7
50 Words / 7 Steps

The
Holy Bible

The Blessed Book
or
Just another book
??????

E. L. "Eddie" Taylor

The Blessed Book
Table of Contents

Dr. Luke to Theophilus

Fulfilling of Malachi 3:1

Fulfilling of Isaiah 7:14

Revealed to Joseph

Birth of John the Baptist

Birth of Jesus

Record of John the Baptist

Holy Bible; unlike any other book

In chapter one of the Gospel according to St. Luke, Dr. Luke begins the book with the first four verses being a statement in his purpose for writing to The-oph-i-lis.

In verses one and two, Dr. Luke states,

Forasmuch as many have taken in hand to set forth in order a declaration of those things which are most surely believed among us, even as they delivered them unto us, which from the beginning were eyewitnesses, and ministers of the word.

Dr. Luke is stating here that it is not his intent to try and add to that which has already been delivered, for those who were eyewitnesses and ministers of the Word have already set in order, a declaration of those things most surely believed among them.

Dr. Luke was inspired to write to the need of affirming and witnessing to its truths, of which has now taken place in supernatural ways, yet came to pass according to Holy Scripture.

We can read of Dr. Luke's intent and purpose for writing to The-oph-i-lus in verses three and four.

It seemed good to me also, having had perfect understanding of all things from the very first, to write to thee in order, most excellent Theoph-i-lus, that thou mightiest know the certainty of those things, wherein thou hast been instructed.

Dr. Luke had for himself the excellence of knowledge to live a life by faith, through the love, grace and mercy of the one true Triune God; God the Father, God the Son, God the Holy Ghost.

And just as Dr. Luke wrote to The-ophi-lus, that he might know of the certainties of those things most surely believed among them, his inspired writing of the Gospel would also apply to us today as it reveals the events that have taken place.

As we look at chapters one and two, we will see the fulfilling of prophecy concerning the coming Messiah and how they are fulfilled in the life of Jesus Christ.

Before we look at verses 5-25 of chapter one, it may be well for us to read once again the prophecy given by Malachi (Mal a kai) in chapter three, verse one, some four hundred years earlier.

Behold, I will send my messenger, and he shall prepare the way before me; and the Lord, whom ye seek, shall suddenly come to his temple, even the messenger of the covenant, whom ye delight in; Behold, he shall come, saith the Lord of host.

Now, let us take a look at the gospel of St. Luke 1:5-25 to see how that some four hundred years after this prophecy, in the fullness of the timing of the Lord God, it is now coming to pass.

Let us look to its unfolding.

There was in the days of Herod, the king of Judea, a certain priest named Zacharias, of the course of A-bi-a: and his wife was of the daughters of Aaron, and her name was Elisabeth.
And they were both righteous before God, walking in all the commandments and ordinances of the Lord blameless.

And they had no child, because that Elisabeth was barren, and they both were now well stricken in years.
And it came to pass, that while he executed the priest's office before God in the order of his course, according to the custom of the priest's office, his lot was to burn incense when he went into the temple of the Lord.
And the whole multitude of the people was praying without at the time of incense. And there appeared unto him an angel of the Lord standing on the right side of the altar of incense.
And when Zach-a-ri-as saw him, he was troubled, But the angel said unto him, Fear not, Zacharias: for thy prayer is heard; and thy wife Elisabeth shall bear thee a son, and thou shalt call his name John. And thou shalt have joy and gladness; and many shall rejoice at his birth, for he shall be great in the sight of the Lord, and shall drink neither wine nor strong drink; and he shall be filled with the Holy Ghost, even from his mother's womb.

And many of the children of Israel shall he turn to the Lord their God. And he shall go before him in the spirit and power of E-li-as, to turn the hearts of the fathers to the children, and the disobedient to the wisdom of the just; to make ready a people prepared for the Lord.

And Zach-a-ri-as said unto the angel, Whereby shall I know this? For I am an old man, and my wife well stricken in years. And the angel answering said unto him, I am Gabriel, that stand in the presence of God; and am sent to speak unto thee, and to shew thee these glad tidings.

And, behold, thou shalt be dumb, and not able to speak, until the day that these things shall be performed, because thou believest not my words, which shall be fulfilled in their season.

And the people waited for Zach-a-ri-as, and marveled that he tarried so long in the temple. And when he came out, he could not speak unto them: and they perceived that he had seen a vision in the temple: for he beckoned unto them, and remained speechless.

And it came to pass, that, as soon as the days of his ministration were accomplished, he departed to his own house.

And after those days his wife Elisabeth conceived, and hid herself five months, saying, Thus hath the Lord dealt with me in the days wherein He looked on me, to take away my reproach among men.

As we pause a moment to reflect, it is now some four hundred years since Malachi (3:1) prophesied:

Behold, I will send my messenger, and he shall prepare the way before me: and the Lord whom ye seek, shall suddenly come to his temple, even the messenger of the covenant, whom ye delight in:
Behold; he shall come, saith the Lord of hosts.

Here we can see the time is now at hand for the coming of the Messiah; In the fullness of the timing of God, the Lord God has sent the angel Gabriel, to announce to Zach-a-ri-as that he and his wife Elisabeth, shall have a son; although they are both well on in years, that he shall be called John; that he shall prepare the way of the Lord.

The announcement has been made, and it is now the sixth month for Elisabeth to be with child, and the angel Gabriel is now about to be sent to see the virgin Mary, as we can read in verses 26-38

And in the sixth month the angel Gabriel was sent from God unto a city of Galilee, named Nazareth, to a virgin espoused to a man whose name was Joseph, of the house of David; and the virgin's name was Mary.
And the angel came in unto her, and said, Hail, thou that art highly favored, the Lord is with thee; blessed art thou among women. And when she saw

him, she was troubled at his saying, and cast in her mind what manner of salutation this should be.

And the angel said unto her, Fear not, Mary: for thou hast found favor with God. And, behold, thou shall conceive in thy womb, and bring forth a son, and shall call his name JESUS.

He shall be great, and shall be called the Son of the Highest: and the Lord God shall give unto Him the throne of his father David: And He shall reign over the house of Jacob forever; and of his kingdom there shall be no end.

Then said Mary unto the angel, How shall this be, seeing I know not a man?

And the angel answered and said unto her, The Holy Ghost shall come upon thee, and the power of the Highest shall overshadow thee: therefore also that holy thing which shall be born of thee shall be called the Son of God.

And, behold, thy cousin Elizabeth, she hath also conceived a son in her old age: and this is the sixth month with her, who was called barren. For with God nothing shall be impossible.

And Mary said, Behold the handmaid of the Lord; be it unto me according to thy word. And the angel departed from her.

Again, we want to pause for a moment. We can see Elisabeth is six months with child, although she is beyond child bearing years; The child she carries is to be called John, and is to prepare the way of the Lord. Now the angel Gabriel has made a visit to the virgin Mary, and has told her she has found favor with God, that she would conceive a son, though knowing not a man, and shall call his name Jesus, that He shall be called the Son of God.

When she replied, how can this be? Seeing I know not a man, the angel answered and said unto her how it would be, that nothing is impossible with God.

And the angel gave Mary an example by revealing unto her that her cousin Elisabeth, who was beyond child bearing years, was now six months with child.

And Mary replied, be it unto me according to thy word. Mary still did not understand, but she no longer needed to understand, she just needed to be willing. If this is to be, then God will have to be in the arrangements, The Lord God will bring it to pass, therefore if this is to be so, then let it be so unto me.

The Lord God does not force His will upon any of us, but when we are willing by faith, to be obedient, the Lord our God then allows for us to become an instrument of His master plan to redeem us. Now, the prophecy foretold some seven hundred years earlier (in Isaiah 7:14) Therefore the Lord Himself shall give you a sign; Behold, a virgin shall conceive, and bear a son, and shall call his name (Immanuel.) *this prophecy is now about to fulfill, the angel departs from Mary and Mary departs to see her cousin Elisabeth as we can read in verses 39-49.*

And Mary arose in those days, and went into the hill country with haste, into a city of Judah; and entered into the house of Zach-a-ri-as and saluted Elisabeth.

And it came to pass, that, when Elisabeth heard the salutation of Mary, the babe leaped in her womb; and Elisabeth was filled with the Holy Ghost; And she spake out with a loud voice, and said, blessed art thou among women, and blessed is the fruit of thy womb. And whence is this to me that the mother of my Lord should come to me?

For, lo, as soon as the voice of thy salutation sounded in my ears, the babe leaped in my womb for joy. And blessed is she that believed; for there shall be a performance of those things which were told her from the Lord.

And Mary said, my soul doth magnify the Lord, and my spirit hath rejoiced in God my Savior. For He hath regarded the low estate of His handmaiden: for, behold, from henceforth all generations shall call me blessed. For He that is mighty hath done to me great things; and holy is His name.

Again as we pause to reflect, Mary and Elisabeth do not understand all that is going on with them, or why they have been chosen to be an instrument of God's plan.

But this one thing they did know, God was in the midst of what was happening.
How else could Elisabeth conceive a son, when she is beyond child bearing years?
How else could Mary conceive a son, when knowing not a man?

As we can read in verse 56
And Mary abode with her about three months, and returned to her own house.

Those three months must have been very exciting and precious times to Mary and Elisabeth. Would it not have been great to somehow have been there and seen and heard their joy and bewilderment in their sharing and caring for one another?
But now, Mary has returned to her own house, and whether or not it was when Mary returned home, that Joseph, her husband to be, begin to ponder as to what he would do, or whether the angel Gabriel had already revealed to Joseph in a dream that it was alright to take Mary as his wife, this we do not know, but we can read in Matthew, 1:18-25, and see that God does prepare and reveal to hearts to receive by faith, and yet not by a blind faith, but a trusting faith in God. Let us now take a look at Matthew 1:18-25.
But before we do, let us look at the prophecy foretold some 700 years earlier in Isaiah 7:14. Therefore the Lord himself shall give you a sign; Behold, a virgin shall conceive, and bear a son, and shall call his name Immanuel.

Now, on to Matthew 1:18-25 as the prophecy begins to fulfill.

Now the birth of Jesus Christ was on this wise: When as His mother Mary was espoused to Joseph, before they came together, she was found with child of the Holy Ghost.

Then Joseph her husband, being a just man, and not willing to make her a public example, was minded to put her away privily. But while he thought on these things, behold, the angel of the Lord appeared unto him in a dream, saying, Joseph, thou son of David, fear not to take unto thee Mary thy wife; for that which is conceived in her is of the Holy Ghost.

And she shall bring forth a son, and thou shalt call his name JESUS: for He shall save His people from their sins.

Now all this was done, that it might be fulfilled which was spoken of the Lord by the prophet, saying, behold, a virgin shall be with child, and shall bring forth a son, and they shall call his name Emmanuel, which being interpreted is, God with us.

Then Joseph being raised from sleep did as the angel of the Lord had bidden him, and took unto him his wife: And knew her not till she had brought forth her firstborn son: and he called his name JESUS

And now let us return to St. Luke 1:57-80

Now Elisabeth's full time came that she should be delivered; and she brought forth a son. And her neighbors and her cousins heard how the Lord had shewed great mercy upon her, and they rejoiced with her. And it came to pass, that on the eighth day they came to circumcise the child; and they called him Zach-a-ri-ah, after the name of his father. And his mother answered and said, Not so; but he shall be called John. And they said unto her, there is none of thy kindred that are called by this name.

And they made signs to his father, how he would have him called. And he asked for a writing table, and wrote, saying, His name is John.

And they marveled all. And his mouth was opened immediately, and his tongue loosed, and he spake, and praised God. And fear came on all that dwelt round about them: and all these sayings were noised abroad throughout all the hill country of Judea.

And all they that heard them laid them up in their hearts, saying, what manner of child shall this be! And the hand of the Lord was with him.

And his father Zach-a-ri-as was filled with the Holy Ghost, and prophesied, saying, Blessed be the Lord God of Israel; for He hath visited and redeemed His people, And hath raised up an horn of salvation for us in the house of his servant David; As He spake by the mouth of His holy prophets, which have been since the world began:

that we should be saved from our enemies, and from the hand of all that hate us;

To perform the mercy promised to our fathers, and to remember His holy covenant; The oath which He sware to our father Abraham, that he would grant unto us, that we being delivered out of the hand of our enemies might serve Him without fear, in holiness and righteousness before Him, all the days of our life.

And thou, child, shalt be called the prophet of the Highest: for thou shalt go before the face of the Lord to prepare His ways; To give knowledge of salvation unto His people by the remission of their sins, through the tender mercy of our God; whereby the dayspring from on high hath visited us, to give light to them that sit in darkness and in the shadow of death, to guide our feet into the way of peace.

And the child grew, and waxed strong in spirit, and was in the deserts till the day of his showing unto Israel.

Let us pause once again; The Lord God has sent the angel Gabriel to Zach-a-ri-as, to say unto him, that he and his wife Elisabeth shall have a son, even though they both are now well on in years. Their son has now been born.

The angel Gabriel has come unto Mary, to say unto her that she shall conceive, and bear a son, though she knows not a man, she shall name him JESUS, and He shall be called the Son of God. The angel Gabriel then reveals unto Joseph in a dream to fear not in taking Mary to be his wife, for that which is conceived in her is of the Holy Ghost as foretold by the prophet.

We have read of the event of the birth of Jesus already taking place in the gospel of Matthew 1:18-25. It gives the detail of the angel Gabriel revealing to Joseph the prophecy that was foretold 700 years earlier by the prophet Isaiah in Isaiah 7:14.

Now we read of the same event of the birth of Christ as it is recorded in the gospel of Luke to give more information on the event that is to take place in Bethlehem.

The forerunner has now been born to prepare the way of the Lord. The virgin birth of Jesus has been announced and now about to come to pass, and He shall be born in Bethlehem as foretold some five hundred years earlier in Micah 5:2 which reads;

But thou, Bethlehem Eph-ra-tah, though thou be little among the thousands of Judah, yet out of thee shall He come forth unto me that is to be ruler in Israel; whose goings forth have been from of old, from everlasting.

We can read of this now fulfilling some five hundred years later in Matthew 2:1 and Luke 2:1-7.

Matt. 2:1- Now when Jesus was born in Bethlehem of Judea in the days of Herod the king, behold, there came wise men from the east to Jerusalem.

Luke 2:1-7 And it came to pass in those days, that there went out a decree from Caesar Augustus, that all the world should be taxed. (and this taxing was first made when Cy-re-ni-us was governor of Syria.) And all went out to be taxed, everyone into his own city.

And Joseph also went up from Galilee, out of the city of Nazareth, into Judea, unto the city of David, which is called Bethlehem; (because he was of the house and lineage of David.) to be taxed with Mary his espoused wife, being great with child.

And so it was, that, while they were there, the days were accomplished that she should be delivered.

And she brought forth her firstborn son, and wrapped Him in swaddling clothes, and laid Him in a manger; because there was no room for them in the inn.

The forerunner John the Baptist, has now been born. The Lord Jesus Christ, the Son of God, has been born of virgin birth. He was born in the city of Bethlehem. All three of these events came to pass in the way they were foretold hundreds of years earlier.

Now let us go to the gospel according to St. John for more on the life of John the Baptist, the one who is to prepare the way of the Lord; and also look unto the Lord Jesus Christ; the Lamb of God. We can begin at verses 6, 7, and 8 of St. John, chapter one.

There was a man sent from God, whose name was John, the same came for a witness, to bear witness of that light, that all men through him might believe.

He was not that light, but was sent to bare witness of that light. *(In vs. 15)* John bare witness of Him and cried, saying, this was He of whom I spake, He that cometh after me is preferred before me: for He was before me.

(We can read of that in vs. one and two)

In the beginning was the Word, and the Word was with God, and the Word was God. The same was in the beginning with God. *(in vs. 14)* And the Word was made flesh, and dwelt among us, (and we beheld His glory, the glory as of the only begotten of the Father,) full of grace and truth. (vs. 18) No man has seen God at any time; the only begotten Son, which is in the bosom of the Father, He hath declared Him.

We can then read the record of John in versus 19-37

And this is the record of John, when the Jews sent priests and Levites from Jerusalem to ask him, who art thou? And he confessed, and denied not; but confessed, I am not the Christ. And they asked him, what then? Art thou Elias? And he saith, I am not. Art thou that prophet? And he answered no.

Then said they unto him, who art thou? That we may give an answer to them that sent us, what sayest thou of thyself?

John said, I am the voice of one crying in the wilderness, make straight the way of the Lord, as said the prophet E-sai-as.

And they which were sent were of the Pharisees. And they asked him, and said unto him, why baptizes thou then, if thou be not that Christ, nor E-li-as, neither that prophet? John answered them saying, I baptize with water: but there standeth one among you, whom ye know not; He it is, who coming after me is preferred before me, whose shoe latchet I am not worthy to unloose. These things were done in Beth-ab-a-ra beyond Jordan, where John was baptizing. The next day John seeth Jesus coming unto him, and saith, Behold the Lamb of God, which taketh away the sin of the world. This is He of whom I said, after me cometh a man which is preferred before me: for He was before me. And I knew Him not: but that He should be made manifest to Israel, therefore am I come baptizing with water.

And John bare record, saying, I saw the Spirit descending from heaven like a dove, and it abode upon Him. And I knew Him not: but He that sent me to baptize with water, the same said unto me, upon whom thou shalt see the Spirit descending, and remaining on Him, the same is He which baptizeth with the Holy Ghost.

And I saw, and bare record that this is the Son of God. Again the next day after John stood, and two of his disciples; And looking unto Jesus as He walked, John said, Behold the Lamb of God! And the two disciples heard John speak, and they followed Jesus.

These are but three of the prophecies that we have touched upon; the forerunner, John the Baptist, the virgin birth, and Bethlehem, the city where Jesus was born.

There are many other prophecies, foretold, fulfilled, in the Holy Bible concerning the life, death, burial, and Resurrection, in the life of Jesus Christ here on earth such as being sold for thirty pieces of silver, mocked and spit upon, bruised and battered, yet not a bone of His body was broken.

He would be crucified with malefactors, yet be buried with the rich, and then... the glory of it all!

On the third day the tomb would be empty;
He would not be there!
The tomb is empty! He is risen!
He lives! He is Lord!

We can see the Holy Bible is unlike any other book ever written. Many who see the Holy Bible to be just another book, full of fairy tales and fables, will have to wrestle with this question, if they seek for truth, how could men write in the manner of which these men wrote, and have it all come together hundreds of years later, in the one solitary life of Jesus Christ, as prophecy fulfilled in Him according to the scriptures?

We can believe the Holy Bible through a substance of faith, or perceive it as foolishness, the choice is ours to make.
But the choice should not be made with indifferent thought. Choices we make in this life, determined the pathway of the journey of this life, and to our eternal destiny.
We need to be aware to the substance of our choices; our hopes; and of our faith, for a faith of some kind is a part of all of us; whether a true faith or a misguided faith. We can look deeper into faith at another time, Lord willing, but for now we want to say this, the Holy Bible speaks to us in Hebrews 11:6, that without faith in God, it is impossible to please Him.
When we place our trust in God with all our heart, even when this life is unfair; even when we do not understand all the trials and adversities of life.
We then, by faith, can still cast all our cares on Him, for we know that He careth for us.

It is then, we have of His peace, not as the world giveth but the peace that passeth our reasoning; the peace that passeth understanding.

It is His perfect love that carries us through our fears. It is through Him that we overcome, and are more than conquerors.
It is because of the substance for our faith that it abounds within our belief system.
In the gospel of St. John 14:1 the Lord Jesus has this to say, Let not your heart be troubled: ye believe in God, believe also in me.

Chapter 17:3 We can read, And this is life eternal, that they may know Thee, the only true God, and Jesus Christ, whom Thou hast sent.
Many questions arise each day about the Holy Bible; Is it the Blessed Book... or just another book? Is it the infallible Word of God... or fairy tales and fables?
Am I not sure what I believe the Holy Bible to be? God has created us with freewill to choose, but our choices do not change the Holy Bible from what it is. But our choices will change us for the better, or for the worse, as we travel this journey of life.
And of the many questions that confront us in the trials of this life; one of the most often asked is this...
How can the Holy Bible be the infallible Word of God, when written by men?

This is offered for consideration,
Yes, men did write down the words of the Holy Bible, but as giving answer to whether or not it could be the infallible Word of God because of that, raises at least two other questions...

First, could men write in this manner, out of their own understanding, and have it come to pass as prophesied hundreds of years earlier?
And the second question is this, if they could have written the words out of their own understanding, would they have not given man more of the credit? Would they not have wanted more of the glory?
And we can take it a step farther, how likely could it be that forty different men, over a period of some fifteen hundred plus years, living in different times, coming out of different backgrounds, and having different vocations, bring together into one theme, The redemptive love of God, with saving grace, for all of mankind, that whosoever will believe on the only begotten Son of GOD as Savior and Lord, shall not perish but have eternal life with Him.
For all of this to come together in this manner, to shine forth out of darkness into the life of Jesus Christ and His coming according to prophecy of scripture, and shine light upon the purpose of His coming on behalf of mankind, would take an equation that goes far beyond our greatest mathematical comprehension.

It needs to involve a higher power. It does involve a higher power. The Holy Spirit of God authored the Holy Bible, as He inspired men to write.

We have looked with a very quick overall view of the Holy Bible and now may ask of ourselves;

Do I believe the Holy Bible to be the Blessed Book, the infallible Word of God, or do I choose to see it in a lesser light, as just another book?

If one is not yet quite sure what to believe, we can also take a look at the Gospel Message that comes forth from the Holy Bible, and do it with fifty words intertwined into seven steps.

This is also true with faith; how do we define faith? How do we obtain faith? Faith can also be answered in an overall view of fifty Words within seven steps.

Each of the three can stand on their own merit, but when we intertwine the three together, we can have an even better understanding for ourselves, and also be able to give a more clear and simplified answer to those who ask for the reason of hope within us, for living our lives as we do.

O Lord, our Lord, how excellent is Thy name in all the earth! who hast set thy glory above the heavens. (Psalms 8:1)

To God be the glory!

Great things, He hast done!

Amen.

Section III

The Gospel Message

What does it mean?

Through *50/7*?

Table of Contents

Overall View

6 Days

Day 7

Freewill to fall

Good News

Choice of Journey

Notes

Let us pause to ask of self can I answer with an overall view of the Gospel Message in the same manner as giving answer on The Holy Bible?

Can we then take those 50 words, and intertwine them into 7 steps, and share the 50 words through each step?

The fifty words can be shared within a minute. Add another minute or two and references can be given for the seven steps.

Then if more time is available and the interest is there, conversation can be shared one with the other for the opportunity that is open.

We will be able to take ourselves to the scriptures to affirm that of which we believe. It will also enable us to share with others, as opportunities open themselves.

50/7 helps to provide the clearest and most simplified answer we can, and many of our own opinions will then be left unsaid

Here are 50 words that may be used in answer for an overall view of the Gospel Message.

An overall view of **The Gospel Message** *in 50 words.*

In the beginning GOD.
All things were made by Him.
GOD created man in the image of GOD.
GOD created man with freewill to choose.
All have sinned and come short.
The wages of sin is death.
But the gift of GOD is eternal life through Jesus Christ our Lord.

The 7 Steps can then intertwine with the 50 Words in this manner.

Step (1) - In the beginning GOD.
                Genesis 1:1 and St. John 1:1, 2

Step (2) - All things were made by Him.
                St. John 1:3 and Genesis 1:1-27

Step (3) - GOD created man in the image of GOD.
                Genesis 1:26; 2:7; 2:21, 22; 1:27

Step (4) - GOD created man with freewill to choose.
                Genesis 2:15-17; 3:1-7

Step (5) - All have sinned and come short.
                Genesis 3:8-14; Romans 3:23

Step (6) - The wages of sin is death.
                Gen. 3:15-24; Romans 6:23a

Step (7) - But the gift of GOD is eternal life through Jesus Christ our Lord
                Romans 6:23b; 5:8; St. John 3:16

As we are now ready to take an overalll view of the Gospel Message through 50 words in 7 steps, I would like to share one more thought for your consideration.

There is in the Holy Bible that which is called the law of (referring back) or (in reference to) this does not take away or add to the Word, but provides added detail to that which has already occurred or has been stated. For example, Genesis 2:4-25 refers back to chapter one of Genesis to provide added detail.

So we have Genesis 1:1 to 2:3 which gives information of God in the beginning creating the heaven and the earth in six days and the seventh day of rest, then Genesis 2:4-25 is information that provides added detail to the information already given in chapter one.
The continuation of events taking place after chapter 2:3 of Genesis takes up again at 3:1.

We can see this more clearly as we go through the steps. Now, as we open our Bibles; beginning with step one, we can read in Gen. 1:1 and St. John 1:1, 2

Then as we continue with step two and go forward, we will bring verses of chapter two into chapter one at various places which is added information as to how GOD created all things and made man in the image of GOD.

As we begin, also keep this in mind, when reading from this book, all type that is in regular New Times Roman is as written in the Holy Bible, that which is in Italic type are my own comments for your consideration.

Let us begin....

Overall view of the Gospel Message

(including the law of referring back)

Step one - *In the beginning GOD*
Gen. 1:1; St. John 1:1, 2

In the beginning GOD created the heaven and the earth.

In the beginning was the Word, and the Word was with GOD, and the Word was GOD, the same was in the beginning with GOD.

Step two - *All things were made by Him*
St. John 1:3; Gen. 1:2-27

All things were made by Him; and without Him was not anything made that was made.

And the earth was without form, and void; and darkness was upon the face of the deep.

And the Spirit of God moved upon the face of the waters.

In Genesis 1:3-27
We can find the things that GOD has made in the six days of creation.

Day 1 - vs. 3,4,5

And GOD said, Let there be light: and there was light. And GOD saw the light, that it was good: and GOD divided the light from the darkness. And GOD called the light Day, and the darkness He called Night.

And the evening and the morning were the first day.

Day 2 - vs. 6,7,8

And GOD said, Let there be a firmament in the midst of the waters, and let it divide the waters from the waters. And GOD made the firmament, and divided the waters which were under the firmament from the waters which were above the firmament: And it was so. And GOD called the firmament Heaven. And the evening and the morning were the second day.

Day 3-vs. 1:9, 10, 11; *2:5, 6;* 1:12,13

And GOD said, Let the waters under the heaven be gathered together unto one place, and let dry land appear: and it was so.

And GOD called the dry land Earth; and the gathering together of the waters called He Seas. And GOD saw that it was good.

And GOD said, Let the earth bring forth grass, the herb yielding seed. And the fruit tree yielding fruit after his kind, whose seed is in itself, upon the earth; And it was so.

Let us pause here for a moment, to insert verses 5, and 6 of chap. 2 into chap. 1, between verses 11 and 12 to provide added information to the 3rd day of creation.

We can see this law of referring back more clearly a little later on, for now, let us read again vs. 11 of chap. 1, then bring in vs. 5 and 6 of chap. 2, then return to chap. 1 and read vs. 12 and 13 to conclude Day 3 of creation.

(Gen.1:11)

And GOD said, Let the earth bring forth grass, the herb yielding seed, and the fruit tree yielding fruit after his kind, whose seed is in itself, upon the earth: and it was so.

(2:5,6)   And every plant of the field before it was in the earth, and every herb of the field before it

grew; for the Lord GOD had not caused it to rain upon the earth, and there was not a man to till the ground, But there went up a mist from the earth, and watered the whole face of the ground.
(1:12,13) And the earth brought forth grass, and herb yielding seed after his kind, and the tree yielding fruit, whose seed was in itself, after his kind: and GOD saw that it was good.

And the evening and the morning were the third day.

Day 4 - vs. 14-19

And GOD said, Let there be lights in the firmament of heaven to divide the day from the night;
And let them be for signs, and for seasons, and for days and years: and let them be for lights in the firmament of the heaven to give light upon the earth: and it was so.
And GOD made two great lights; the greater light to rule the day, and the lesser light to rule the night: He made the stars also.
And GOD set them in the firmament of the heaven to give light upon the earth, and to rule over the day and over the night, and to divide the light from the darkness: and GOD saw that it was good.
And the evening and the morning were the fourth day.

Day 5 - vs. 20-23

And GOD said, Let the waters bring forth abundantly the moving creature that have life, and fowl that may fly above the earth in the open firmament of heaven.

And GOD created great whales and every living creature that moveth, which the waters brought forth abundantly after their kind, and every winged fowl after his kind: And GOD saw that it was good.

And GOD blessed them, saying, be fruitful and multiply, and fill the waters in the seas, and let fowl multiply in the earth.

And the evening and the morning were the fifth day.

Day 6 - vs. 1:24,25; 26, 2:7,8,9; 15,-17; 19,20; back to 18, forward to 21-23; then 1:27-30; 2; 4 and 25; back to 1:31

And GOD said, Let the earth bring forth the living creature after his kind, cattle, and creeping thing, and beast of the earth after his kind: and it was so.

And GOD made the beast of the earth after his kind, and cattle after their kind, and every thing that creepeth upon the earth after his kind: and GOD saw that it was good.

Before we go on to vs. 26, I want to let you know that we want to insert vs. 7,8, and 9; 15, 16, and 17; 19,20; back to 18, forward to 21-23; of chap. 2 between the verses of 26 and 27 of chapter one. In doing so we will have the added information as to how GOD made man(2:7) and woman (2:21,22) how GOD created man with freewill to choose (2:15-17). If at a later time, you do not wish to insert the verses of chapter two into chapter one between vs. 26 and 27 you can at least remind yourself that most of chapter two refers back to chap. 1, to bring forth added detail.

It is the Word of GOD revealing more detail to the Word of God. If we do not have this understanding, we may become confused when reading 2:5 that there was not a man to till the ground, when we had just read in 1:26,27 that GOD has created man. But as was earlier said, 2:5 brings information into the third day of creation, while vs.1:26,27 speak of the 6th day.

Again, this is scripture adding detail to that which has already taken place in scripture. Let us now read 1:26, then chapter 2:7,8,9, and onward before returning to 1:27.

We will then have a better understanding of steps 3 and 4.

Step 3 - *GOD created man in the image of GOD.*
Gen.1:26, 27; 2:7; 2:21,22

Step 4 - *GOD created man with Freewill.*
Gen. 2:15-17; 3:1-7

Let us now see how it unfolds.

(Gen. 1:26)
And GOD said,
Let us make man in our image, after our likeness: and let them have dominion over the fish of the sea, and over the fowl of the air, and over the cattle, and over all the earth, and over every creeping thing that creepeth upon the earth.

(2:7,8, and 9) And the Lord GOD formed man of the dust of the ground, and breathed into his nostrils the breath of life; and man became a living soul.

And the Lord GOD planted a garden eastward in Eden; and there He put the man whom he had formed.

And out of the ground made the Lord GOD to grow every tree that is pleasant to the sight, and good for food; the tree of life also in the midst of the garden, and the tree of knowledge of good and evil.

(15-17) and the Lord GOD took the man, and put him into the garden of Eden to dress it and to keep it.

And the Lord GOD commanded the man, saying, of every tree of the garden thou mayest freely eat: but of the tree of the knowledge of good and evil, thou shall not eat of it: for in the day that thou eatest thereof, thou shalt surely die.

(19,20) And out of the ground the Lord GOD formed every beast of the field, and every fowl of the air; and brought them unto Adam to see what he would call them: and what so ever Adam called every living creature, that was the name thereof.

And Adam gave names to all cattle, and to the fowl of the air, and to every beast of the field: but for Adam there was not found an help meet for him, (18) and the Lord GOD said, It is not good that the man should be alone; I will make him an help meet for him.

(21,22,23) And the Lord GOD caused a deep sleep to fall upon Adam, and he slept; and He took one of his ribs, and closed up the flesh instead thereof and the rib, which the Lord GOD had taken from man, made He a woman, and brought her unto the man.

And Adam said, this is now bones of my bones, and flesh of my flesh: she shall be called Woman, because she was taken out of man. (1:27-28) so GOD created man in his own image, in the image of GOD created He him. Male and Female created He them.

And GOD blessed them, and said unto them, Be fruitful, and multiply, and replenish the earth, and subdue it: and have dominion over the fish of the sea, and over the fowl of the air, and over every living thing that moveth upon the earth.

As we pause here a moment to reflect, we can see what happens between 1:26 and 27; how GOD created man (2:7) and woman (2:21,22) how GOD gave man the freewill to choose, (2:15-17)
Now as we continue with 1:29, 30 we can see how GOD continues to reveal to Adam and his wife, His blessing and instruction to them. We then bring in 2:4 and 24,25 of chapter 2 then return to chapter 1:31 to conclude the sixth day. Chapter 2 vs. 1,2, and 3 speaks of the 7th day. We then continue at chapter 3:1.

(Gen. 1:29, 30)
And GOD said, Behold, I have given you every herb bearing seed, which is upon the face of all the earth, and every tree, in the which is the fruit of a tree yielding seed; to you it shall be for meat.

And to every beast of the earth, and to every fowl of the air, and to every thing that creepeth upon the earth, wherein there is life, I have given every green herb for meat. And it was so.

(2:4) These are the generations of the heavens and of the earth when they were created, in the day that the Lord GOD made the earth and the heavens.
(24,25) Therefore shall a man leave his father and his mother, and shall cleave unto his wife:

And they shall be one flesh. And they were both naked, the man and his life, and were not ashamed.

(1:31)   And GOD saw everything that He had made, and behold, it was very good. And the evening and the morning were the 6th day.

Day 7 - vs. 2:1,2, and 3

Thus the heavens and the earth were finished, and all the host of them. And on the seventh day GOD ended His work which He hath made;

And He rested on the seventh day from all His work which He had made. And GOD blessed the seventh day, and sanctified it: because that in it He had rested from all His work which GOD created and made.

Let us pause here before going on to chapter 3:1 of Genesis, we can see that four of the seven steps and the overall view of the Gospel Message have now taken place.

(1)-In the beginning GOD
(2)-All things were made by Him
(3)-GOD created man in the image of GOD
(4)-GOD created man with freewill.

In chapter three, we will find steps five, and six, now let us once again reflect as to where we are at this place in scripture.

The Lord GOD has created a vast universe and a glorious earth. The Lord GOD has created man in the image of GOD that man might have fellowship with the Lord GOD;

The Lord GOD created a bountiful and a wondrous supply for man in the Garden of Eden, it was pleasant to the sight and good for food. Life was beautiful, life was good, and life was abundant.

Man had a sinless, guilt-free, unashamed relationship with the Lord GOD, our heavenly Father. Only the tree of the knowledge of good and evil was there to come between GOD and man, the tree was there to give man the choice to choose GOD or the other. Everything else was there for them to freely partake of and enjoy the pleasures thereof. Now let us continue with Genesis 3:1-7, and see how the temptation to sin takes place even though the Lord GOD was making full provision for man with plenteous and gracious living.

(Gen. 3:1-7) NOW the serpent was more subtil than any beast of the field which the Lord GOD had made. And he said unto the woman, Yea, hath GOD said, ye shall not eat of every tree of the garden?

And the woman said unto the serpent, we may eat of the fruit of the trees of the garden: But of the fruit of the tree which is in the midst of the garden, GOD hath said, ye shall not eat of it, neither shall ye touch it, lest ye die.

And the serpent said unto the woman, ye shall not surely die: for GOD doth know that in the day ye eat thereof, then your eyes shall be opened, and ye shall be as gods, knowing good and evil.

And when the woman saw that the tree was good for food, and that it was pleasant to the eyes, and a tree to be desired to make one wise, she took of the fruit thereof, and did eat, and gave also unto her husband with her; and he did eat. And the eyes of them both were opened, and they knew that they were naked; And they sewed fig leaves together, and made themselves aprons.

Let us pause and reflect for a moment upon this thought that, in the midst of all that the Lord GOD is providing, we can survey the joy of His goodness; the wealth of fellowship they had with Him; the unsearchable riches found in Him.

The Lord GOD is a bountiful supply, with all this wondrous glory, how could anyone even be tempted to sin? Well, the temptation to sin has now been made. And both, Adam and the woman have taken of the temptation to sin.

They were deceived with half-truths; they were not told the whole truth, they did not rightly divide the truth, they did not consider the consequences, they did not count the cost of sin.

We too, are very apt to sin if we lean unto our own understanding. Let us take a closer look at what has taken place with Adam and Eve and see what it can also reveal unto us.

First, as we look at 3:1 we can read where The Holy Bible tells us that the serpent was more subtil than any beast of the field. That begs this question of us...how do we perceive the devil to be? Do we see him to be, or not to exist? Do we see him in a red suit with horns and a pitchfork? Maybe we see him for more of who he is...as one who is more subtil, more cunning, more deceitful; maybe we already know him to be a liar, and that he is the father of lies.

He is very cunning in getting us to acknowledge as to what we know GOD has said to us in the knowing of doing right or wrong. Then when the devil has us aware of truth, he deceives with half-truths, to tempt us to be, or continue to be, disobedient toward GOD.

When we are aware of truth, the devil simply shrugs it off and replies with half-truths; he does not tell the whole truth. When we are aware of truth, the devil simply shrugs and says, you will not surely die, but you're eyes will be opened, and you shall be as other gods, knowing both good and evil. He told them the truth up to a point; he just did not tell them the whole truth.

When he told them that their eyes would be opened, they were opened. But he did not tell them of the cost that comes through guilt, shame, and separation.

When he told them they would know both good and evil, they did. He just did not tell them of the consequences of their choice in being disobedient toward the Lord GOD. There is a terrible price to be paid for sin.

Sin is deeply rooted into three sources. All temptations come forth from the three, and all temptations can be traced back to one or more of the three sources. And the three sources are:
(1)-The lust of the flesh   (2)-The lust of the eyes
(3)-The pride of life

We can see all three of these taking place with Adam and Eve in the garden of Eden, chapter 3 verse 6:

(1)- Eve saw the tree was good for food.
(Lust of the flesh)

(2)- That it was pleasant to the eyes
(Lust of the eyes)

(3)- A tree to be desired to make One wise.
(The pride of life)

We too, are often tempted through one or more of these three sources, they may come with a cunning deceit of different means, but they will come.

We can find them rooted in one or more of the three. And the only way to overcome the temptation is by rightly dividing the truth, looking unto Jesus, and the being lead of the Spirit of GOD.

It is then that we can have a right relationship and fellowship with the Lord GOD.

Now let us continue at 3:8 and see the terrible cost that must be paid for sin.
(Gen. 3:8-24)

And they heard the voice of the Lord GOD walking in the garden in the cool of the day: and Adam and his wife hid themselves from the presence of the Lord GOD amongst the trees of the garden. And the Lord GOD called unto Adam, and said unto him, Where art thou?

And Adam said, I heard Thy voice in the garden, and I was afraid, because I was naked, and I hid myself.

And the Lord GOD said, Who told thee that thou were naked? Hast thou eaten of the tree whereof I commanded thee that thou shouldest not eat?

And Adam said, the woman whom Thou gavest to be with me, she gave me of the tree, and I did eat.

And the Lord GOD said unto the woman, What is this that thou hast done? And the woman said, the serpent beguiled me, and I did eat. And the Lord GOD said unto the serpent, Because thou hast done this, thou art cursed above all cattle, and every beast of the field; upon thy belly shalt thou go, and dust shalt thou eat all the days of thy life: and I will put enmity between thee and the woman, and between thy seed and her seed; it shall bruise thy head, and thou shalt bruise his heel.

Unto the woman the Lord GOD said, I will greatly multiply thy sorrow and thy conception; in sorrow thou shalt bring forth children; and thy desire shall be to thy husband, and he shall rule over thee.

And unto Adam the Lord GOD said, Because thou hast hearkened unto the voice of thy wife, and has eaten of the tree, of which I commanded thee, saying, thou shalt not eat of it: cursed is the ground for thy sake; In sorrow thou shalt eat of it all the days of thy life; the thorns also and thistles shall it bring forth to thee; and thou shall eat of the herb of the field; in the sweat of thy face shalt thou eat bread, till thou return unto the ground; for out of it were thou taken: for dust thou art, and unto dust shalt thou return.

And Adam called his wife's name Eve; because she was the mother of all living. Unto Adam also and to his wife did the Lord GOD makes coats of skins, and clothed them.

And the Lord GOD said, behold, the man is become as one of us, to know good and evil: And now, lest he put forth his hand, and take also of the tree of life, and eat, and live forever.

Therefore the Lord GOD sent him forth from the garden of Eden, to till the ground from whence he was taken.

So the Lord GOD drove out the man; and the Lord GOD placed at the east of the garden of Eden, Cherubims, and a flaming sword which turned every way, to keep the way of the tree of life.

As we pause once again, let us think upon this thought. The Lord GOD created in all his creation, the means to reproduce within itself after its own kind

The grass and the herbs yielding seed after its kind; The fruit tree, after its kind whose seed is in itself, every living creature that moveth which the waters brought forth abundantly after their kind, every winged fowl after his kind; And the earth to bring forth every living creature after his kind; Cattle, and creeping thing, and beast of the earth after their kind.

And the Lord GOD created man in the image of GOD, and GOD gave to man the means to be fruitful, and multiply, and replenish the earth, and subdue it.

Yes, the Lord GOD created in all of His creation of earth, the seed within itself to reproduce after its own kind

Now, the seed of Adam is a seed tarnished with sin. The tarnished seed of Adam will reproduce after its own kind. All mankind of Adam seed will now be conceived in sin with Adam nature.

Man is now born with the nature to know both, good and evil. He will exalt self through self-pride; he will see himself as self sufficient; looking to please self through the lust of the flesh; the lust of the eyes, and believing he is entitled to do so.

Therefore, all mankind, being born of Adam seed, has come short of the glory of GOD. Man's eyes are opened to the lust of the flesh, the lust of the eyes, and the pride of life.

Man is opened to self-glory; to self-pride; he knows both good and evil, right and wrong. Instead of bringing forward a right relationship with GOD. there is guilt, shame, and deceit that dwells within man. Man will try to cover up sin, he will try to deny sin, he will try to blame someone else, or something else.

Man will try and justify sin in some way; or he may even deny there is the Lord GOD rather than confess and repent of sin.

The Holy Bible tells us in Romans 3:23 that all have sinned and come short of the glory of GOD. And in Rom. 6:23a that the wages of sin is death. We know that sin keeps us from right relationship with the Lord GOD.

So where is the good news?
It is... Rom. 6:23b

But the gift of GOD is eternal life through Jesus Christ our Lord.

It is... Rom. 5:8
But GOD commendeth His love toward us, in that, while we were yet sinners, Christ died for us.

It is... St. John 3:16
For GOD so loved the world that He gave His only begotten Son, that whosoever believeth in Him should not perish, but have everlasting life.

It is... St. John 17:3
And this is life eternal, that they might know Thee the only true GOD, and Jesus Christ, whom Thou hast sent.

It is ... Looking unto Jesus, the author and finisher of our faith;

It is ... In knowing, the substance of our hope; our faith, that in which we place our confidence, our trust, our hope, our reliance.

It is ... In knowing, how Jesus Christ came according to prophecy of Holy Scripture, and the purpose for which He came;
That through the virgin birth, provided by the overshadowing of the highest, enabled the Lord Jesus to have a sinless birth. One not conceived through the tarnished seed of Adam, after its own kind, but one that is of a sinless birth. Born of above, through Jesus Christ our Lord.

That whosoever believes on Him for paying our sin debt shall know pardon and forgiveness of sin, and shall not perish but have everlasting life.

The Heavenly Father; The Lord our GOD, has prepared the way. He has sent His only begotten Son into the world, to die for the sins of whosoever will receive Him.

The Lord Jesus Christ; the Son of GOD, has opened up the way; He is the living Word

In the beginning was the Word, the Word was with GOD, the Word was GOD, the same was in the beginning with GOD.

The Word was made flesh, and dwelt among us, and we beheld His glory, (the glory as of the only begotten of the Father,) full of grace and truth. No man hath seen GOD at any time; the only begotten Son, which is in the bosom of the Father, He hath declared Him. (St. John 1:1, 2; 14, 18)

The Holy Ghost; the Comforter, The Spirit of God sent to dwell with us and be within us. To lead us into truth and righteousness; to empower and enable us for the days in which we live. As we travel this journey of life, we can look upon the life of Jesus Christ here on earth, and behold His glory:

Behold the man:
   and find substance for our faith,
     find hope for despair,
       find victory over defeat,
        find joy over sorrow,
          as we behold His glory.

And we not only have hope, but we know life eternal, and have life more abundantly. Yes, the virgin birth was prophesied 700 years before it came to pass. (Isaiah 7:14)

His birth in Bethlehem, foretold 500 years before it came to pass. (Micah 5:2)

The forerunner to prepare the way of the Lord, prophesied 400 years before it came to pass. (Malachi 3:1)

Many other prophecies are fulfilled in the life of Christ here on earth concerning His life, death, burial, and Resurrection.

Here are a few of the many:

He was sold for thirty pieces of silver; He was battered and bruised; Mocked and reviled, yet not a bone of His body was broken; He was crucified with malefactors, yet He was buried with the rich. He was led as a lamb to the slaughter, but He opened not His mouth to defend Himself But that which sets Him apart from all others is this;

On the third day after His crucifixion and burial, early in the morning, the tomb is EMPTY!

He Lives!
He is Risen!

He was crucified, buried, and arose the 3rd day according to Holy Scripture.

After His Resurrection:

He was seen of Cephas, then of the twelve; after that He was seen of above five hundred brethren at once; after that He was seen of James; then of all the apostles. (I Corinthians 15:5-7)

Yes, now is Christ risen from the dead and become the first fruits of them that slept. Since by man came death, by man came also the resurrection of the dead. For as in Adam all die, even so in Christ shall all be made alive. (I Corinth. 15:20-22)

All of us have some knowledge, in one way or another; some even have greater knowledge, through the knowledge of man and the ways of the world, but excellence of knowledge comes in knowing Christ as Lord and Savior, In knowing the oneness of the Triune GOD.

To know Him! ... The Lord Jesus; ... to learn more of Him, helps us apply His teachings and examples to our lives, through the enabling power of the Holy Spirit.

To acknowledge Him in all our ways, to trust the Lord GOD with all our heart, to love the Lord GOD with all our soul, to rely upon the Lord GOD with all our strength, however weak or strong that strength may be.

The inner joy of the Lord, to be our strength, brings forth a perfect love to cast out our fears. It will help us to know, we are more than conquerors through Christ the Lord

That we have celebration of life with victories through Jesus Christ our Lord, who loves us, who gave Himself for us, who one day will come again and receive unto Himself all who have received Him by faith believing.

For those who are trusting in Him, know He will keep them against the day of judgment, while those who know Him not will hear Him say depart from me.

Yes, nothing shall be able to separate us from the love of GOD, which is in Christ Jesus, our Lord.

This is the good news of the Gospel Message, to believe in Christ, to receive Him into our heart and soul and live life through Him. It is life eternal! and joy unspeakable! FOREVER more! But while we are here, we can grow in a loving, living relationship with the Lord GOD that goes far beyond the magnitude of words.

<u>It is a life</u> lived through Him.

<u>It is a life</u> of unsearchable riches found in Him.
(a wonderful peace)
(a perfect love from above)

<u>It is a life</u> fulfilled through Him.

It is joy <u>unspeakable</u> and full of glory in knowing Him

It is <u>life eternal</u>, and more; it is the abundant life to be lived. It is GOOD NEWS!

It is life through:
<u>The One</u> who is the same yesterday today, and forever more.

<u>The One</u> who gives to all that believe in Him, the promise of His return, to receive us unto Himself that where He is, there we may be also. FOREVER!

<u>The One</u> who is ever faithful and able to light our path for the journey home by the way of the cross.

<u>The One</u> in whom the Lord our GOD, commanded the light to shine out of darkness, hath shined in our hearts, to give the light of the knowledge of the glory of GOD in the face of Jesus Christ.

<u>The One</u> whom GOD has sent; the one who was willing to pay the price of sin, (wages of sin is death) to redeem us back to the Father, though His love, grace, and mercy.

<u>The One</u> who is the way, the truth, and the life, the one in whom no one can come to the Father except by Him.

GOD has now commandeth all men everywhere to repent: Because He hath appointed a day, in the which He will judge the world in righteousness by the one whom He hath ordained; whereof He hath given assurance unto all men, in that He hath raised Him from the dead. (Acts 17:30, 31)

That if thou shalt confess with thy mouth the Lord Jesus, and shall believe in thine heart that GOD hath raised Him from the dead, thou shalt be saved. For with the heart man believeth <u>unto righteousness</u> and with the mouth confession is made unto salvation. (Romans 10:9, 10)

The Pharisee stood and prayed thus with himself, GOD, I thank thee, that I am not as other men are, extortioners, unjust, adulterers, or even as this publican. I fast twice a week, I give tithes of all that I possess.

And the publican, standing afar off, would not lift up so much as his eyes unto heaven, but smote upon his breast, saying, GOD be merciful to me a sinner.

I tell you, this man went down to his house justified rather than the other: for every one that exalted himself shall be abased; and he that humbleth himself shall be exalted. (St. Luke 18:9-14)

Humble yourself therefore under the mighty hand of GOD that He may exalt you in due time: Casting all your care upon Him; for He careth for you. (I Peter 5:6,7)

Jesus said, Come unto me, all ye that labour and are heavy laden, and I will give you rest. Take my yoke upon you, and learn of me; for I am meek and lowly in heart: and ye shall find rest unto your souls. For my yoke is easy, and my burden is light. (Matthew 11:28-30)

This may be a good place to ask of Self What have I done with the one called Jesus? Have I rejected Him, and retained my sins through my own self-righteousness, which are as filthy rags?

Have I, as the Pharisees, retained my sins, depending upon religious works of my own standing, denying that which the Lord GOD has provided through Christ and His righteousness?

What shall I do with this one called Jesus? Who came according to Holy Scripture, with the purpose to reconcile us back to the Father, paying the sin debt for whosoever will believe in Him.

Shall we, or have we, ask Him into our heart and life by the leadership of the Holy Spirit?

The Lord GOD has created us with freewill to choose, the choice we make will determine our eternal destiny.

The love of Father GOD to us, <u>has prepared the way</u> back to Him, as He commendeth His love to us, in that while we were yet sinners, Christ would come to die for us.

The love of the Lord Jesus Christ to us, <u>has opened up the way</u> in that He left the splendor of heaven to do for us what we could not and cannot do for ourselves.

The Holy Spirit of GOD to us, <u>reveals the way</u>. He will reveal the things of Christ to us, He shall not speak of Himself but will guide, those who seek, into all truth.

This is the GOOD NEWS of the Gospel Message.

(St. John 3:16) For GOD so loved the world, that He gave His only begotten Son, that whosoever believeth in Him should not perish, but have everlasting life.

It is my Prayer that our eyes will be opened to know Him, as He walks with us along the way, that our hearts may burn within us, as He talks with us, and opens to us the scriptures, as He did with the two on the road to Em-ma-us. (Luke 24:13-32)

(Romans 11:36)

For of Him, and through Him, and to Him, are all things: to whom be glory forever. Amen.

GOD Bless!

Section IV

??? *50/7* ???
50 Words / 7 Steps

An overall view of

??? *faith* ???

? ? ? ? ? ? ? ? ? ? ? ?

How shall we define Faith???...

? ? ? ? ? ? ? ? ? ? ? ? ? ?

How do we obtain Faith???

? ? ? ? ? ? ? ? ? faith ? ? ? ? ? ? ? ?

? ? ? ? ?   E. L. "Eddie" Taylor

faith   Faith   *faith*

We will now take a closer look at Faith through 50/7. We have looked at the Holy Bible, and the Gospel Message through 50/7.

When we have done so with faith, we will see that each one, although very large subjects, can be applied to 50/7, and that each one can stand on their merit, but when intertwined together, give an even greater inner awareness to what one believes and why they believe in the manner in which they do.

It will be with that greater awareness that one will be able to give an answer to anyone who asks of them, the reason of hope they have within for living life as they live it.

We will also expand farther on 50/7 as a tool for giving witness as to what one believes, and the opportunities, that do and do not, present themselves. And the growth of ease and confidence within as the words are treasured in our hearts, which helps us to apply the steps for living life to the fullest.

Now, let us apply 50/7 to an overall answer on faith, to see how we might define faith? how we might obtain faith?

50/7 on **Faith**

50 words- to define faith...

7 steps- to obtain faith...

Can we have an understanding of faith wherein we can define faith in fifty words or less?

To look up the word faith in a dictionary can give a place to begin, a place where for the most part one can find ready agreement upon which to focus.

To look up the definition of faith in many dictionaries, faith will be defined in this manner. Unquestioning belief anything believed; to have complete trust; where confidence is placed; that in which one can have reliance.

With that as a focus, would it not be fair to say that faith can be in anyone or anything of which we have complete confidence and place our trust fully therein?

And if faith can be in anyone or anything, does that not make faith a very large subject to think upon? In being able to give an answer for faith?

If we have great confidence in someone, would that not cause us to think or say, I have faith in you? If we have placed our trust in something, would that not be based on a substance of some kind of confidence and trust in doing so?

It may be a faith without evidence to support it, because one may place their faith in someone or something out of greed, pride, personalities, or even in what appears to be a good cause. And if faith can be in anyone or anything, does that not cause faith to be a very large subject to think upon?

Do we know the reason for placing trust and confidence into whatever area wherein we have done so? Can we give an answer in fifty words intertwined with seven steps of application, for what ever it is, wherein we have placed our faith?

I would like to share these fifty words for your consideration. You may have a different definition that works best for you.

The main point I wish to make here is the need to bring that which we truly believe into an overall view with the fewest words possible, that a better understanding for self as to what one may believe has more clarity that can also help to give a better answer to anyone who may ask the reason for the faith we have, whatever it may be of that in which we trust.

The fifty words to define faith that I give for you to consider are these:

*Faith is the substance of things hoped for
 the evidence of things not seen.
Faith can be placed in anyone or anything
 wherein we place our confidence;
 put our trust; rely upon.
Faith can sustain us or disillusion us.
Redeeming faith gives substance of hope,
 of life lived in Christ.*

We can now apply the seven steps, intertwined with the fifty words.

Step 1 - *Faith is the substance of things hoped for.* (Hebrews 11:1a)

The key word here is substance; it can give knowledge of the reason for our hope; give a better understanding for that which is believed. We need to diligently seek the reason why we place our confidence and trust wherever that might be.

Step 2 - *Faith is the evidence of things not seen.* (Hebrews 11:1b)

That which is seen by sight is not of faith. We may put our trust and confidence there because of what we see. We base that trust on the substance of knowledge we have in doing so.

Step 3 - *Faith can be in anyone or anything wherein we put our trust; place our confidence.*

We can have varying degrees of knowledge based on education and world experiences, but excellence of knowledge comes with substance of knowledge we have of Christ.

Because at times, for one reason or another, we might find ourselves placing our confidence and trust into someone or something without fully searching out the substance in doing so.

We may not seek for evidence that gives substance to what one may believe.

Step 4 - *Wherever we put our faith, (place our trust; have our confidence) that faith can sustain us, or disillusion us depending upon the outcome.*

Not to be disappointed when faith does not fulfill in ways we believe that it will, brings us two areas for thought.

First, one must be able to deliver all that is promised to the one who has entrusted their faith.

Second, the one who is entrusting their faith needs to have a right understanding of what is promised.

Step 5 - *Redeeming faith gives substance of hope to live life through Jesus Christ, as Lord and Savior:*

To search out the substance of the life of Jesus Christ as fulfilled according to Holy Scripture gives one meaning to weigh choice and make choice through own freewill.

Step 6 - Receiving Christ into heart and life by faith helps one to know he/she is justified through faith. The just shall live by faith and walk in the Spirit and not after the flesh.

The natural man receiveth not the things of the Spirit of GOD: for they are foolishness unto him: neither can he know them, because they are spiritually discerned. (I Corinthians 2:14)

Without faith in GOD it is impossible to please Him; for he that cometh to GOD must believe that He is, and that He is a rewarder of them that diligently seek Him. (Hebrews 11:6)

Step 7 - Learning the oneness of the Triune GOD helps us by faith (through substance of evidence not seen) to live by faith.

To sanctify the Lord GOD in our hearts: and be ready always to give an answer to every man that asked you a reason of the hope that is in you with meekness (being submissive to the will of another) and fear. (to respect the freewill of another to differ)
(I Peter 3:15)

The Holy Spirit can bring forth a teachable spirit, and also an understanding heart from within us, when the submission of the will is to the heavenly Father, and not to the will of another, not even self.

We can then respect the freewill of others to differ, not because we fear them in the term that we may normally give to fear, but that we are aware they have freewill to differ.

The secret things belong unto the Lord our God: but those things which are revealed to us, belong unto us, and to our children forever.
(Deuteronomy 29:29)

What is it that is revealed? – St. John 3:16; Romans 5:8; 6:23. How is it revealed? It is revealed in the Holy Bible, It is revealed by the Holy Spirit of God. It is revealed through the life of Jesus Christ, as He came according to Holy Scripture. And when we know the purpose of His coming, we can go therefore, and teach all nations, baptizing them in the name of the Father, and of the Son, and of the Holy Ghost.

What is it we are to teach?

It is the oneness of the Triune God.

The Oneness of God Triune.

If we have an understanding of the purpose for the Lord GOD being triune, we can share that understanding with others, and leave with them their choice of freewill as to how they will respond.
What does it mean that GOD is three in one and one in three?

If we look at the six days of creation as seen in the Holy Bible; Gen. 1:3-27, we can see there would be no need for GOD to be triune had He not created man with freewill. In verses 3-25, GOD spoke and it was so. GOD said, and He could see that it was good. It is at verse 26 we see the plurality of the oneness of GOD.

GOD said, Let us make man in <u>our</u> image, after <u>our</u> likeness... GOD created man to have fellowship with Him, and to have dominion over all of His creation. The Lord GOD created man with freewill of choice, therefore the Lord GOD knew the fall of man existed.
In His love for mankind, through His mercy, He prepared the way by grace for redemption. Romans 3:23; 5:8; 6:23; St. John 1:1,2;14;18; 3:16; 14:6;11; 17:3

The only begotten Son of GOD, the Lord Jesus Christ, has opened up the way for whoso-

ever will believe in Him shall not perish but have everlasting life.

The Lord Jesus paid the sin debt for all willing to receive Him into their heart and life, desiring to live life through Him.

The Holy Spirit of GOD, (The Holy Ghost) then indwells within to lead into truth and righteousness. To put us in remembrance of whom we are in Christ and to empower us for these days in which we live.

There are three ingredients for redeeming faith; they are substance, evidence, and submission, when they are blended together they bring forth an excellence of knowledge that gives excellence of knowledge to faith. A voluntary surrender of self-will in knowing GOD is working for our eternal good, that nothing is impossible for Him to accomplish, that He can deliver us, but whether or not He does so is not to be according to our will, for we yet will trust Him and put our confidence in Him, knowing He takes all things and works them together for good to them that love Him and are the called according to His purpose.

Redeeming faith has two areas in order for faith to be complete and beneficial.

The first deals with intellect; the mind. We all have knowledge in one way or another, and some have greater knowledge through teachings of man *and ways of the world, but excellence of knowledge comes in knowing Christ.*

With the mind we can think, believe, and know, certain things. To say I think this or I think that on any subject can have with it a pretty strong conviction. But to say I believe this, brings with it a stronger conviction. And yet when we can say I know, then that carries with it the strongest of convictions.

We can with our mind think that Christ came to die for us and has the power to raise from the dead, we may even believe it to be so and therefore have stronger conviction, and for some they may even know and know that they know, and still be deceived into thinking their faith is complete. But the devil and his angels believe and yet tremble knowing they are not in right relationship with the Lord GOD.

The second area of redeeming faith comes within the heart. With the mind we can hear the Word preached and know it goes forth in power; the Word brings forth substance, the life of Christ brings forth evidence, but we must bring forth freewill of self surrender from the heart.

This second area that comes forth from the heart is done with repentance.

Which means knowing self for whom and what we are and desiring for the Lord God to create in us a clean heart; to change our way of thinking and behavior? We can hear the word, believe it to be true, and for whatever reason receive it not into the heart, (such as the rich young ruler in St. Luke 18:22-25) therefore still be lost; separated from right relationship with GOD. For with the heart man believeth unto righteousness; and with the mouth confession is made unto salvation. It is with own freewill that one will receive or reject into the heart and life which the Lord God has made provision of reconciliation for whosoever will receive the Lord Jesus Christ and the finished work of the cross.

Faith at times may appear to us to be weak, other times strong; faith may seem vivid, other times vague. Sometimes mysterious, unsettling, while at other times a quite strength. Because of the many variations, faith may often find us in quite a dilemma. That is unless we have a substance for our hope and a right understanding on which to stand.

Looking unto Jesus as the author and finisher of our faith; as we look at His life here on earth and see how He came according to Holy Scripture; as we learn of Him and His purpose for coming. We find evidence of things not seen. We can cast all our cares on Him because we know He cares for us. That even when life is unfair, chaotic, full of troubles, we can know of His peace within, not peace as the world giveth, but His peace, a peace that comes forth in His love to cast out our fears.

The substance of life found in the life of Christ at His birth; burial; and Resurrection.

The Holy Bible that reveals to us a roadmap of substance that brings forth Blessed Hope.

The Holy Spirit that reveals, teaches, and leads in substance of truth.

The key word for having faith is not faith itself but <u>substance</u> of knowledge in having trust and confidence beyond our understanding of it all. With trust and confidence:

Acknowledge GOD in all our ways.
Trust GOD with all our heart.
Love GOD with all our soul.
Rely on GOD with all our strength,
great or small;   weak or strong.

We might feel intimidated when thinking of the full surrender of self because we know ourselves well enough that the word <u>all</u> will cause us to come short of meeting that commitment all the time and we do not want to be hypocritical. But there is one place where the word all fits very nicely, I can do all things through Christ who strengthens me.

Jesus came unto His own and His own received Him not, but as many as received Him gave He power to become the sons of God.

It is hard for us to comprehend why the Lord God would commit the message of the Gospel to a handful of disciples who at the time of their decision to follow Jesus, were very immature.

One had said to Jesus, Lord I will die for you. Only for him to hear his Lord say unto him, before this night is over you will deny me three times before the cock crows.

Two others had asked of Jesus if they might sit at His side in glory, one on the right the other on the left. Jesus replied, you know not what you ask.

Another when he had seen the multitude, asked of Jesus, how can we feed so many with so little? These may be some of the same kind of things we might say today.

But Jesus did not ask them about their knowledge nor did He even ask them about their ability. Jesus simply asked this as a bottom line question. "Lovest thou me." This is where it all begins, it is the foundation upon which we are to build. If we come to Him for any other reason than out of love for Him, we shall miss out on the greatest of all blessings here on earth.

If we come to Him out of love for Him, it will be because we know He first loved us, and gave Himself for us. It is then we know what a friend we have in Jesus. And when we have this kind of knowledge, it is then:

We can learn:
- ☐ *how to deal with difficulties*
- ☐ *how to acknowledge circumstances*
- ☐ *how to overcome*

We can have:
- ☐ *peace that passes understanding*
- ☐ *perfect love to cast out fears*
- ☐ *excellence of knowledge that puts life in proper perspective*
- ☐ *not only life eternal, but life more abundant*

We can do:
- ☐ *all things well through Christ*
- ☐ *the ministry of reconciliation with the leadership of the Holy Spirit*
- ☐ *that which will declare the glory of GOD in our life, through the church, to the world*

Being justified by faith, we have peace with GOD through our Lord Jesus Christ. Looking unto Jesus and seeing the substance of His life bringing forth the evidence to us that can give us the confidence to place our trust in Him.

Therefore the Gospel Message goes forth by Faith through The Word, 50 words, intertwined with 7 steps, The Gospel Message revealed through The Holy Bible, in Faith believing, revealed through the Holy Spirit.

We ask of GOD to create in us a clean heart; a new heart; an understanding heart. A heart that desires to be teachable of the Lord. Through leadership of the Holy Spirit.

Excellence of knowledge:

☐ *gives us great and blessed assurance with substance of hope through that which is found in Jesus Christ as Lord and Savior.*

☐ *That some day...one day... on that day, we shall see Him face to face, and behold His glory and be with Him.*

<u>*Forever*</u>*!*

Let us be ready always, in season and out of season, in times of plenty or in times of want, let us be ready always to share the good news of the Gospel to ourselves within and to others who ask of us the reason of hope we have for living life as we do.

Let us go forward, standing on the promises of almighty God, seeing the privilege that is ours to share in these perilous days, the Lord is at hand and the best is yet to come.

Hallelujah!

*Justified through the cleansing blood
of Christ;*
> *rooted and grounded in His love;*

The Redeemed!
> *And the Redeemed say from
>> the heart...*

Bless the Lord, O my soul:

and all that is within me,

> Bless His Holy name!
>> Amen.

Section V

Now, that we have taken an overall view of The Holy Bible, and the Gospel Message, and Faith through 50/7, let us take...

A closer look at 50/7

Let us quickly summarize as to where we are at this point as we think upon a few thoughts and add a few more that may be of help.

First and foremost we want to bring to mind those thoughts of which we most surely believe we can answer in the fewest words possible.

This will give foundation for what we know and believe for ourselves. We should be able to do that in 50 words or less.

The Holy Bible, the Gospel Message, and Faith are three very large subjects to be able to give an answer of overall view of them.

Many questions are often asked on these three subjects, many kinds of answers and opinions are often given of them.

But each of the three can stand on their own merit. Each of the three can in substance, be narrowed into 50 words to give a foundation for belief, and to be clear with simplicity of answer.

Each of the three can intertwine with the other, to strengthen the knowledge, as to why we believe in the manner that we do, for living our lives in the way that we live them.

And when we have a better understanding for ourselves that if someone should ask of us...

Is the Holy Bible the Blessed Book or just another book? or
What does the Gospel Message mean? or
How do you obtain Faith?

We can then share an answer with them out of a foundation of 50 words. We then can take the 50 words and intertwine them into 7 steps to add substance to our answer and also affirm our own belief.
Once we build a foundation of 50 words for ourselves and take them through the 7 steps...

We can KNOW:
The WHY, of what we KNOW,
HOW to share, of what we KNOW,
and to KNOW, that we KNOW, that we KNOW!

And when we know for ourselves, then our own faith is affirmed and we are able to share with others as opportunities present themselves.

50/7 is only one means of sharing of what we believe.

The main purpose of 50/7 is to bring us toward the narrow form of foundation, to provide with more clarity, a simplified answer so that many of our own opinions will be left unsaid.

We can then share in 50 words, an overall view of the Holy Bible, or in giving a overall answer to The Gospel Message, or defining Faith in 50 words. We can share an answer as short as a minute, or as long as there is interest or somewhere in between, depending on the available time.

By knowing the 50 words, and treasuring them in our hearts, we can affirm them through scripture for ourselves and be able to share to all who should ask of us, the reason of hope within us, for living life as we do.
Therefore the Gospel Message goes forth by Faith through The Word.

50 words... to some, they will just be mere words, without substance to them. They will not be interested in seeking or searching for truths that can be revealed.

For others, they will be words of opinion; they too, will not find any significance in them. They will think or say, that's your opinion and I have mine, therefore they also will not be seeking or searching for truth.

But then for others... they are the wonderful words of life! Yes, there are those who have heard and care not.

But, there are some who have heard and want to hear more. And then, there are those who have heard and now see, and care very deeply.

They will find ways to share 50/7. It may be wearing a 50/7 lapel pin or a cameo necklace. Or it may just simply be to use 50/7 in a form of conversation.

There will be some who will be too busy with other things to even notice, they will quickly dismiss 50/7 from there thoughts or curiosity, they have other things to think about, other things to do, that seem more important to them, whatever those things may be.

It would be to no avail to speak with such a person at that time. If you should approach them, they will only say "I don't have time now," or "I have to do this," or "I have to do that."

There will be some who will notice 50/7 and still not ask about it... they may be too shy, they may think you already believe they know what 50/7 means, and they don't want you to think they are foolish for asking. There may be some other reason for them not to ask even though they have notice 50/7. If we see such a reaction from them, we may, or we may not, ask a question of them at that time.

But there will be others who will quickly, and with much interest, ask, "What does 50/7 mean?" and because we have learned and can be yet learning, we can affirm the answer from within a foundation of 50 words for ourselves and then quickly share with those who ask "What does 50/7 mean?" and then share with them for as long as time and/or interest allow.

It is then we can share, out of our own heart that which we have affirmed and know the why of what we believe for self and for sharing the reason of hope that is within for living life as we live it.

Once again I would like to say that 50/7 can be attainable at ones' own pace, in whatever way works the best for each.

Here is one way of suggestion, that may be of help.

1- Read all three subjects at least once before picking one. Read them as often as needed, until you can pick one of greater interest.

2- Then write down for yourself, the 50 words of overall view, that pertain to that subject. Write the words on something you can carry with you at all times. (small paper or index card)

3- Read the words as often as you can each day, without trying to memorize them. Whenever you can, read them aloud to yourself. You can read the 50 words two or three times within a minute or so, so read them often and before you know it, you will have them memorized without even trying to do so.

4- Read the 7 steps aloud to yourself, (so you become comfortable saying and hearing the words to the steps.)

5- Then take one step at a time, (for as long as it takes) to get familiar with where the step ties in with the 50 words. Go through each step until it is comfortable within you as to where it can be easy to share in conversation.

6- Record the 50 words and 7 steps onto a cassette or cd, then play to yourself often, make notes of any thoughts that come to you as you hear the tape or disc.

7- Once you feel comfortable with the subject chosen, then go to one of the other two, and repeat *the steps. Come back to the first subject and review by reading the words or listening to the tapes at least once a week for awhile, as you study the other subjects.*

Again, this may seem to overwhelm, but it does not need do, you can work at your own pace and in your own way. And whatever length of time it may take, will make it worthwhile in the ease and confidence it then brings forth from within.

That whenever someone should ask of you, The Holy Bible, is it the blessed Book? Or just another book? Or the Gospel Message, what does it mean? Or Faith, how do we define faith? how do we obtain faith?
Best of all, we can know for self, and then you can give answer to anyone who ask of you the reason of hope you have within, as you have narrowed to 50 words and applied the 7 steps into your own heart, and treasure them there, for whenever someone may ask, "50/7 what does it mean?"

It is upon my heart, that if anyone should like to have a Seminar Class. on any, or all, of the three subjects through 50/7, Lord willing, I will try to help in anyway I can.

If you have questions or comments on 50/7, or if you would like more information on 50/7 or seminar sessions, please phone or E-mail:

*Ed "Eddie" Taylor
Ph- 304-727-2762
E-mail - <u>Efiftywords@suddenlink.net</u>*